3 0183 02965 3787

W9-DGJ-985

NEWTON PUBLIC LIBRARY
100 S. VAN BUREN
NEWTON, ILLINOIS 62448

Art Smart

How to Draw Pets

Christine Smith

For a free color catalog describing Gareth Stevens' list
of high-quality books and multimedia programs,
call 1-800-542-2595 (USA) or 1-800-461-9120 (Canada).
Gareth Stevens Publishing's Fax: (414) 225-0377.
See our catalog, too, on the World Wide Web: http://gsinc.com

Library of Congress Cataloging-in-Publication Data

Smith, Christine (Christine Hunnikin)
    How to draw pets / by Christine Smith.
        p. cm. --(Art smart)
    Includes index.
    Summary: Provides simple instructions for drawing nine different pets,
including a fish, a kitten, and a horse.
    ISBN 0-8368-1610-2 (library binding)
    1. Pets in art--Juvenile literature. 2. Drawing--Technique--
Juvenile literature. [1. Pets in art. 2. Animals in art.
3. Drawing--Technique.]
I. Title. II. Series.
NC783.8.P46S6 1996
743'.6--dc20   95-53868

First published in North America in 1996 by
Gareth Stevens Publishing, 1555 North RiverCenter Drive,
Suite 201, Milwaukee, Wisconsin, 53212, USA.
Original © 1993 by Regency House Publishing Limited
(Troddy Books imprint), The Grange, Grange Yard, London,
England, SE1 3AG. Text and illustrations by Christine Smith.
Additional end matter © 1996 by Gareth Stevens, Inc.

All rights to this edition reserved to Gareth Stevens, Inc.
No part of this book may be reproduced, stored in a retrieval
system, or transmitted in any form or by any means, electronic,
mechanical, photocopying, recording, or otherwise without the
prior written permission of the publisher except for the inclusion
of brief quotations in an acknowledged review.

Printed in the United States

2 3 4 5 6 7 8 9 99 98 97

Gareth Stevens Publishing
MILWAUKEE

Materials

Drawing pencils have letters printed on
them to show the firmness of the lead.
Pencils with an *H* have very hard lead.
Pencils with an *HB* have medium lead.
Pencils with a *B* have soft lead. Use
an *HB* pencil to draw the outlines
in this book. Then use a *B* pencil
to complete the drawings.

This type of pencil sharpener
works well because it keeps
the shavings inside
a container.

Once you have drawn the
outlines on a piece of paper,
place a thinner sheet of
paper over them. Then
make a clean, finished
drawing, leaving out
any unnecessary lines.

Use a soft eraser to make any changes you might want.
Color your drawings with felt-tip pens, watercolors,
crayons, or colored pencils.

Shapes

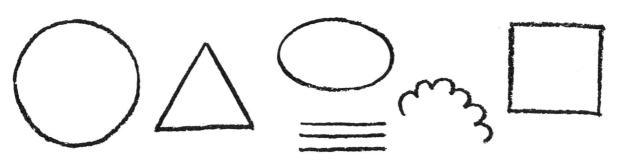

Before you begin drawing, practice the shapes above. Draw them over and over again. All the drawings in this book are based on these simple shapes.

Color

Mixing colors is fun whether you are using colored pencils or paints. Mix red and yellow to make orange. Mix blue and yellow to make green. Red and blue make purple.

An important thing to remember when you're drawing a baby animal is that the head is quite large compared with the body. Notice how the head of this chick and the head of this hen are about the same size.

Look carefully at the animals you see. Sketch them on paper, and make a note of their colors and any special markings they may have.

4

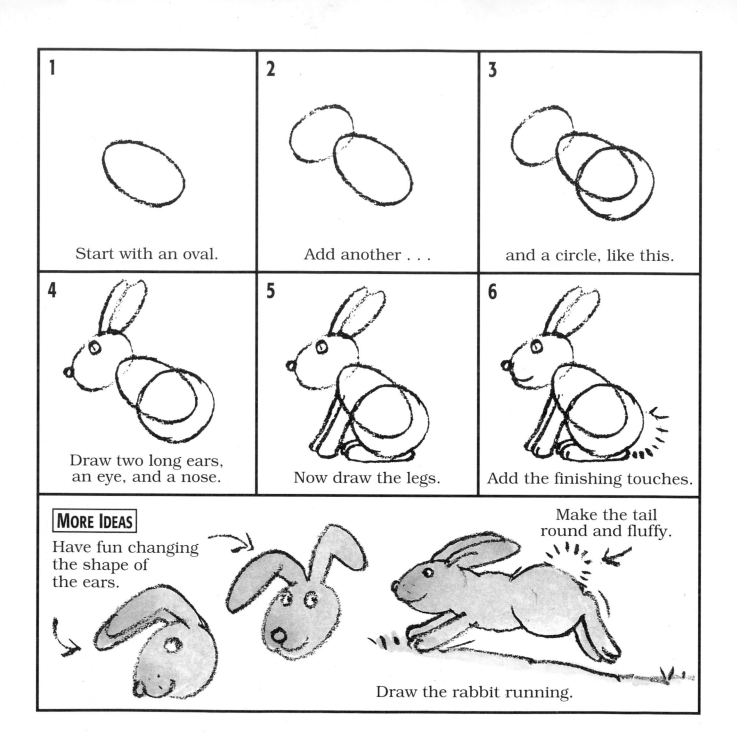

1 Start with an oval.

2 Add another . . .

3 and a circle, like this.

4 Draw two long ears, an eye, and a nose.

5 Now draw the legs.

6 Add the finishing touches.

MORE IDEAS

Have fun changing the shape of the ears.

Make the tail round and fluffy.

Draw the rabbit running.

Rabbit

1 Start with a circle.

2 Add a smaller one.

3 Now join them to make a neck.

4 Add an eye, a beak, and a wing.

5 Draw legs, like this.

6 Add the finishing touches.

MORE IDEAS

Draw some chicks, too.

Draw the chicken pecking.

Draw in the feathers, like this.

8

Chicken

NEWTON PUBLIC LIBRARY
100 S. VAN BUREN
NEWTON, ILLINOIS

1 Start with a circle.

2 Draw front legs, like this.

3 Add ears and a back end.

4 Draw eyes and a nose . . .

5 cheeks and a tail.

6 Add the finishing touches.

MORE IDEAS

It's fun to put the dots of the eyes in different places.

Make the paws round.

Trace the outline of your first drawing to make a back view.

Kitten

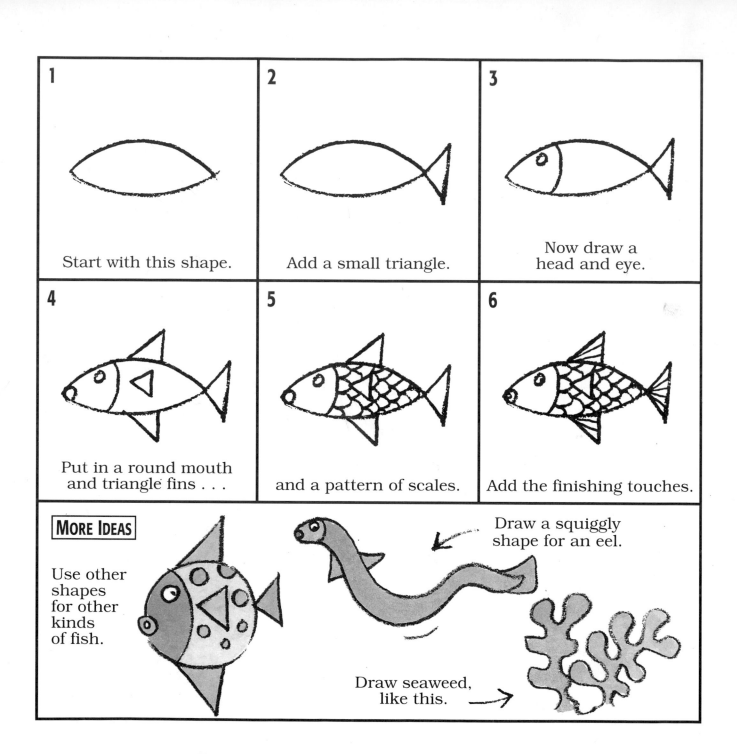

1

Start with this shape.

2

Add a small triangle.

3

Now draw a
head and eye.

4

Put in a round mouth
and triangle fins . . .

5

and a pattern of scales.

6

Add the finishing touches.

MORE IDEAS

Use other
shapes
for other
kinds
of fish.

Draw a squiggly
shape for an eel.

Draw seaweed,
like this.

Fish

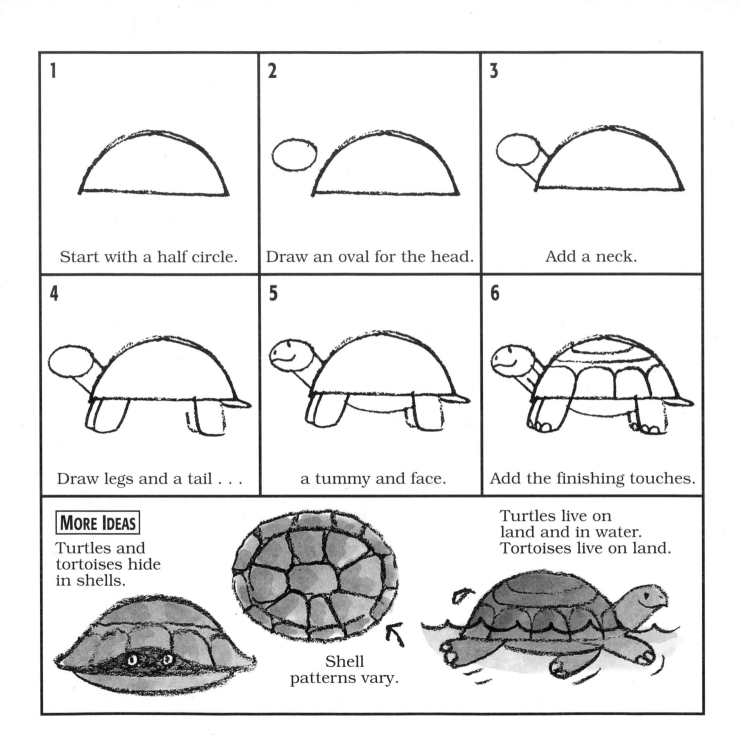

1 Start with a half circle.

2 Draw an oval for the head.

3 Add a neck.

4 Draw legs and a tail . . .

5 a tummy and face.

6 Add the finishing touches.

MORE IDEAS

Turtles and tortoises hide in shells.

Shell patterns vary.

Turtles live on land and in water. Tortoises live on land.

Turtle

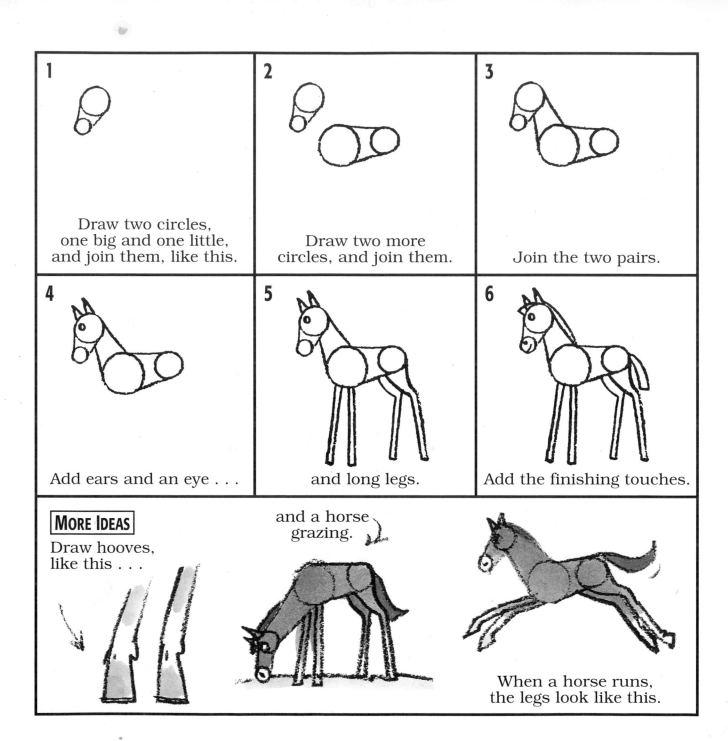

1 Draw two circles, one big and one little, and join them, like this.

2 Draw two more circles, and join them.

3 Join the two pairs.

4 Add ears and an eye . . .

5 and long legs.

6 Add the finishing touches.

MORE IDEAS

Draw hooves, like this . . .

and a horse grazing.

When a horse runs, the legs look like this.

Horse

1 Start with an oval.

2 Add a circle at one end.

3 Draw another circle inside the first circle.

4 Add eyes, ears . . .

5 legs, and a curly tail.

6 Add the finishing touches.

MORE IDEAS

Draw some pigs in various positions.

Try a side view, like this.

18

Pig

1 Start with a circle.

2 Add a larger half circle . . .

3 a beak, and a tail.

4 Draw legs, like this.

5 Draw an eye and a wing.

6 Add the finishing touches.

MORE IDEAS

Draw the bird in flight.

and coming in for a landing.

Draw the bird on a perch . . .

Bird

1 Start with two circles.

2 Then draw an oval.

3 Add a nose and mouth.

4 Draw ears and eyes.

5 Then draw legs.

6 Add the finishing touches.

MORE IDEAS
Change the eyes for a different expression.

Draw a few spots.

Then sit the puppy down.

Puppy

More Books to Read

Animal Crafts. Worldwide Crafts (series). (Gareth Stevens)
Animal Friends. Illa Podendorf (Childrens Press)
The Big Pets. Lane Smith (Viking Children's Books)
Birds. Wings (series). Patricia Lantier-Sampon (Gareth Stevens)
Drawing Cats and Kittens. Paul Frame (Franklin Watts)
Drawing Dogs and Puppies. Paul Frame (Franklin Watts)
Fish Do the Strangest Things. Lenora and Arthur Hornblow (Random)
House Pets. Animals at a Glance (series). (Gareth Stevens)
How to Draw Birds. Barbara Soloff-Levy (Troll)
Look Out for Turtles! Melvin Berger (HarperCollins Children's Books)

Videos

Animal Friends. (Phoenix/BFA Films and Video)
The Animal World. (United Learning)
Animals: Dogs. (Churchill Media)
The Cat. (Barr Films)
The Dog Family. (International Film Bureau)
Dogs, Cats and Rabbits. (Public Media)

Index

NEWTON PUBLIC LIBRARY
100 S. VAN BUREN
NEWTON, ILLINOIS 62448